My United States

Idaho

MELISSA MCDANIEL

Children's Press®
An Imprint of Scholastic Inc.

Content Consultant
James Wolfinger, PhD, Associate Dean and Professor
College of Education, DePaul University, Chicago, Illinois

Library of Congress Cataloging-in-Publication Data
Names: McDaniel, Melissa, 1964- author.
Title: Idaho / by Melissa McDaniel.
Description: New York, NY : Scholastic Inc., [2018] | Series: A true book | Includes bibliographical references
and index.
Identifiers: LCCN 2017056023 | ISBN 9780531235584 (library binding) | ISBN   9780531250778 (pbk.)
Subjects: LCSH: Idaho—Juvenile literature.
Classification: LCC F746.3 .M35 2018 | DDC 979.6—dc23
LC record available at https://lccn.loc.gov/2017056023

Front cover: Tipi near the Sawtooth Mountains
Back cover: Ice climbing at Shoshone Falls

Welcome to Idaho

Find the Truth!

Everything you are about to read is true **except** for one of the sentences on this page.

Which one is **TRUE**?

T or F Idaho produces more potatoes than any other state.

T or F European Americans began settling Idaho in the 1700s.

Find the answers in this book.

Idaho

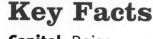

Contents

THE **BIG** TRUTH!

Cutthroat trout

What Represents Idaho?

French fries

Downhill skier

Mountain
bluebird

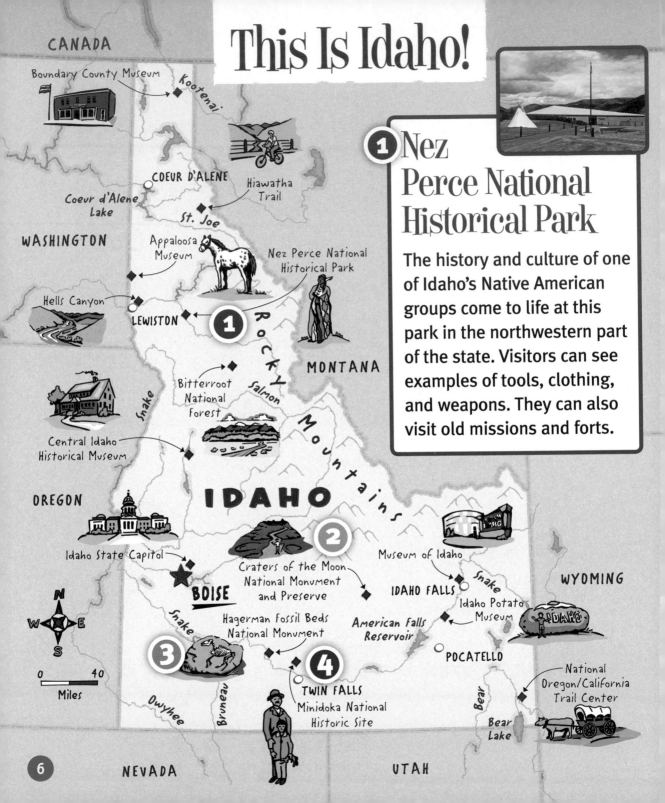

This Is Idaho!

CANADA

Boundary County Museum → Kootenai

COEUR D'ALENE

Coeur d'Alene Lake

Hiawatha Trail

St. Joe

WASHINGTON

Appaloosa Museum

Nez Perce National Historical Park

Hells Canyon

LEWISTON

1

Rocky

MONTANA

Bitterroot National Forest

Salmon

Snake

Central Idaho Historical Museum

Mountains

OREGON

IDAHO

Idaho State Capitol

★ BOISE

Craters of the Moon National Monument and Preserve

2

Museum of Idaho

IDAHO FALLS

Snake

WYOMING

Idaho Potato Museum

Snake

Hagerman Fossil Beds National Monument

3

American Falls Reservoir

POCATELLO

N W E S

0 — 40
Miles

TWIN FALLS

4

Minidoka National Historic Site

Owyhee

Bruneau

Bear

National Oregon/California Trail Center

Bear Lake

1 Nez Perce National Historical Park

The history and culture of one of Idaho's Native American groups come to life at this park in the northwestern part of the state. Visitors can see examples of tools, clothing, and weapons. They can also visit old missions and forts.

NEVADA

UTAH

② Craters of the Moon National Monument and Preserve

Craters of the Moon is a vast lava field in south-central Idaho. It was formed as volcanoes erupted between 15,000 and 2,000 years ago. Today, visitors can explore cooled rivers of lava and lava cones. They can even enter lava tubes—tunnels made of lava.

③ Hagerman Fossil Beds National Monument

Scientists have dug up the remains of many ancient animals at this site in southern Idaho. They include saber-toothed cats, elephant-like mastodons, and horses (pictured).

SOUTH
DAKOTA

④ Minidoka National Historic Site

During World War II (1939–1945), Japanese Americans were forced from their homes and put into camps because people feared they would spy for Japan. About 13,000 people were imprisoned at Minidoka, near Twin Falls. Visitors today can see the remains of the site and learn about its history.

The Sawtooth Mountains contain 57 peaks that are more than 10,000 feet (3,048 meters) tall.

Land and Wildlife

Idaho is wild. Jagged, rocky peaks tower over land that is draped in dark-green forests. There are majestic grasslands, deep canyons, and thundering waterfalls. Cold, clear rivers rush down mountains and across flatlands. This bold landscape shelters thousands of kinds of plants and animals.

The Lay of the Land

Idaho is shaped like an ax. The broad blade of the ax sits in the southern part of the state. Most of this area is flat, rolling grasslands or dry, treeless plains. The Rocky Mountains form much of the handle of the ax. More than 100 Idaho peaks rise above 11,000 feet (3,353 meters). In the northwest, near the Washington border, is a region of gentle hills.

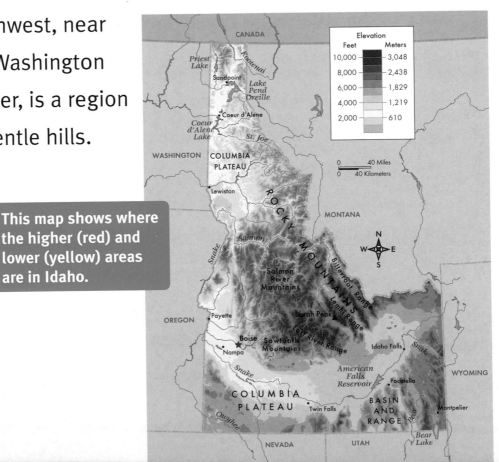

This map shows where the higher (red) and lower (yellow) areas are in Idaho.

Boating on the Snake River is a great way to experience dramatic views of Hells Canyon.

Hells Canyon

The Snake River runs all the way across southern Idaho. Along the Oregon border, it cuts deep into the land, creating Hells Canyon. The canyon likely earned its name because many explorers in the 1800s could not make their way across the rugged land. Hells Canyon is the deepest canyon in North America. In some places, the walls rise 7,900 feet (2,408 m) above the river below. That's even higher than the Grand Canyon in Arizona.

Water tumbles 212 feet (65 m) over the rocky walls of Shoshone Falls.

Water, Water Everywhere

Nearly 9,000 rivers and streams crisscross Idaho. The Snake River is the state's major river. In the middle of its course, the river suddenly rushes over a cliff, forming Shoshone Falls. These roaring falls are even taller than the famous Niagara Falls in New York. Idaho also has thousands of lakes. The largest is Lake Pend Oreille.

Summer and Winter

The climate in Idaho varies greatly from region to region. High in the mountains, winter brings a lot of snow. The snowy mountain slopes attract skiers and snowboarders from around the country. Summers in the mountains are mild. Lower elevations can get hot in the summer, and some areas are very dry. Parts of the southwest are considered deserts. They get less than 10 inches (25 centimeters) of rain per year.

Idaho is home to several major ski resorts.

MAXIMUM TEMPERATURE	MINIMUM TEMPERATURE
118°F	-60°F

Plants

The land in Idaho is a mix of green and brown. Forests cover about 40 percent of the state.

Towering evergreen firs and pines fill these forests. In the flatlands of the south, hardy shrubs such as sagebrush and greasewood are the most common plants. Broad cottonwood trees provide welcome shade along the rivers.

Many types of trees grow in the Sawtooth Mountains.

14

Mountain goats have wide hooves to help them balance on rocky ledges, and they can leap across gaps up to about 12 feet (3.7 m) wide.

Animals

Idaho's northern forests are among the nation's most remote regions. This makes them the perfect home for animals such as grizzly bears and gray wolves. Bighorn sheep and mountain goats climb the rocky slopes. Idaho's many rivers and lakes are clean and cold. Fish such as trout thrive in these waters. High above, eagles, kestrels, and other birds of prey soar in search of a meal.

The name of Boise, Idaho's capital city, comes from a French word meaning "wooded."

Government

When Idaho became a **territory** in 1863, Lewiston was its capital. At the time, gold mining was the biggest industry in Idaho. There were many mines near Lewiston, but they were soon emptied of their valuable resources. Meanwhile, gold had been discovered near Boise in southern Idaho. Miners began heading south, and in late 1864 the capital followed. Boise has been Idaho's capital ever since.

State Government Basics

Idaho's government has three branches. The executive branch carries out the state laws and runs the government. The governor leads this branch. The legislative branch makes laws for the state. It consists of the Senate and the House of Representatives. The state courts make up the judicial branch of government. These courts settle disputes and try people charged with crimes.

IDAHO'S STATE GOVERNMENT

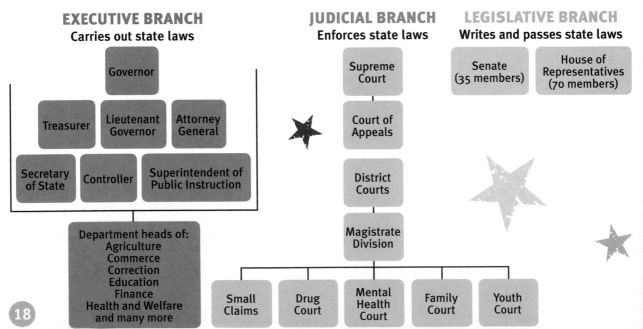

EXECUTIVE BRANCH
Carries out state laws

- Governor
- Treasurer
- Lieutenant Governor
- Attorney General
- Secretary of State
- Controller
- Superintendent of Public Instruction

Department heads of:
Agriculture
Commerce
Correction
Education
Finance
Health and Welfare
and many more

JUDICIAL BRANCH
Enforces state laws

- Supreme Court
- Court of Appeals
- District Courts
- Magistrate Division
  - Small Claims
  - Drug Court
  - Mental Health Court
  - Family Court
  - Youth Court

LEGISLATIVE BRANCH
Writes and passes state laws

- Senate (35 members)
- House of Representatives (70 members)

Some of Idaho's fire departments, which are overseen by county and local governments, use helicopters to help control huge forest fires.

Idaho's Constitution

In 1889, a constitution was written for Idaho, which would become a state the following year. The constitution laid out the basic rules for how Idaho would be governed. The state still follows this same constitution. However, the document has been amended, or changed, more than 100 times. One of the earliest changes, in 1896, gave women the right to vote. Idaho was the fourth state to grant women the vote.

Idaho in the National Government

Each state elects officials to represent it in the U.S. Congress. Like every state, Idaho has two senators. The U.S. House of Representatives relies on a state's population to determine its numbers. Idaho has two representatives in the House.

Every four years, states vote on the next U.S. president. Each state is granted a number of electoral votes based on its number of members in Congress. With two senators and two representatives, Idaho has four electoral votes.

2 senators and 2 representatives

4 electoral votes

With four electoral votes, Idaho's voice in presidential elections is below average compared to other states.

The People of Idaho

Elected officials in Idaho represent a population with a range of interests, lifestyles, and backgrounds.

Ethnicity (2016 estimates)

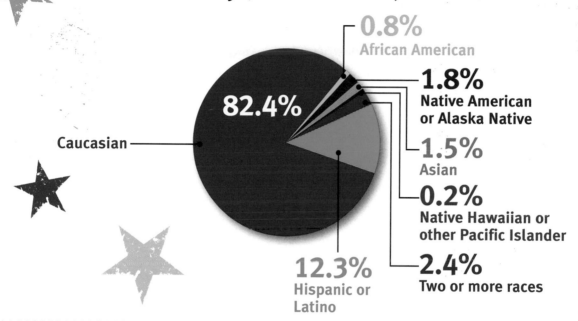

82.4%
Caucasian

0.8%
African American

1.8%
Native American or Alaska Native

1.5%
Asian

0.2%
Native Hawaiian or other Pacific Islander

2.4%
Two or more races

12.3%
Hispanic or Latino

11% speak a language other than English at home.

9% are veterans.

69% own their own homes.

6% were born in another country.

90% graduated from high school.

26% have a bachelor's degree or higher.

THE BIG TRUTH!

What Represents Idaho?

States choose specific animals, plants, and objects to represent the values and characteristics of the land and its people. Find out why these symbols were chosen to represent Idaho or discover surprising curiosities about them.

Seal

Idaho's seal highlights the state's natural resources and beauty. On the right is a miner. The shield in the center shows the Snake River, a pine tree representing forests, and a farmer. Wheat and other crops beneath the shield symbolize the state's agriculture and **horticulture**. The woman on the left represents justice.

Flag

Idaho's flag was adopted in 1907. It shows the state seal against a blue background. Below the seal is a red banner containing the words "State of Idaho."

Cutthroat Trout

STATE FISH
Cutthroat trout thrive in Idaho's cold streams and lakes.

Star Garnet

STATE GEM
From some angles, a delicate white star appears in this deep-purple gem. Northern Idaho and India are the only places in the world where star garnets are found in large numbers.

Huckleberry

STATE FRUIT
Huckleberries are small blue, purple, or red berries that look like blueberries. They are a favorite food of bears.

Western White Pine

STATE TREE
Large stands of western white pine trees grow straight and tall in northern Idaho.

Appaloosa

STATE HORSE
The Nez Perce people were known for riding these spotted, hardworking horses. The breed was first called Palouse, after the region. Later they became known as Appaloosa.

Mountain Bluebird

STATE BIRD
The beautiful mountain bluebird can sometimes be seen hovering above fields, searching for insects to eat.

Explorers Meriwether Lewis and William Clark passed through the Bitterroot Mountains of northern Idaho in 1805.

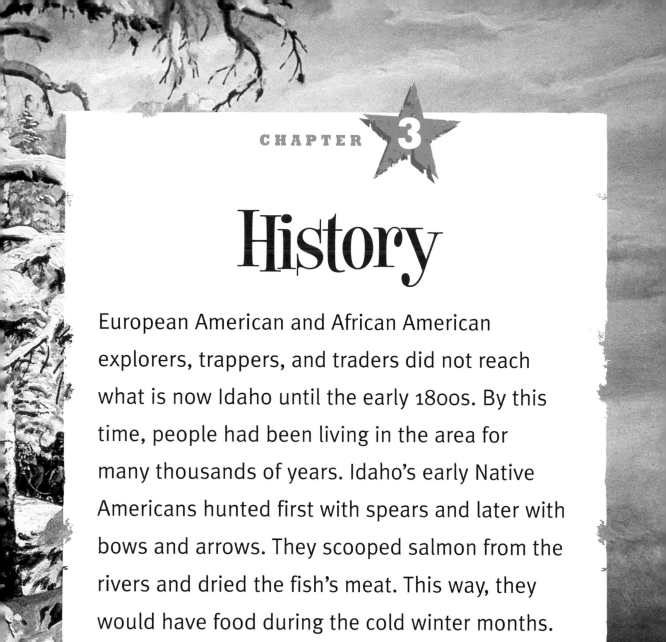

CHAPTER 3

History

European American and African American explorers, trappers, and traders did not reach what is now Idaho until the early 1800s. By this time, people had been living in the area for many thousands of years. Idaho's early Native Americans hunted first with spears and later with bows and arrows. They scooped salmon from the rivers and dried the fish's meat. This way, they would have food during the cold winter months.

Native American Life

Over time, many different Native American cultures arose. The Coeur d'Alene, the Kutenai, and others hunted in the mountains and valleys of northern Idaho. Farther south, the Nez Perce, the Paiute, and the Shoshone lived on the plains. They dug roots from the ground to eat. They hunted animals as small as rabbits and as large as bison. The skins of large animals were used to make **tipis**, which provided shelter.

This map shows some of the major tribes that lived in what is now Idaho before Europeans came.

Hoofbeats

Around 1700, life changed for the people of Idaho. Horses had long been extinct in North America. However, Spaniards brought them from Europe. Some horses escaped from Spanish settlements to the

The Nez Perce became well-known for breeding especially high-quality horses.

south of Idaho. Over time, they wandered north, and Native Americans captured them. The Nez Perce and Shoshone peoples quickly adapted to life on horseback. The horses made hunting bison and other creatures easier.

Strangers From the East

In the early 1800s, newcomers began arriving from the East. A group led by Meriwether Lewis and William Clark passed through the region in 1805. They were exploring the West all the way to the Pacific Ocean. In the years after Lewis and Clark, a few fur traders and **missionaries** arrived in what is now Idaho. Many of them traveled along the famous Oregon Trail, a route leading from the East to Oregon. But for the most part, the land was left to the Native Americans.

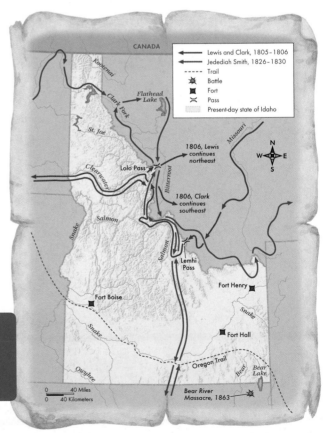

This map shows routes Europeans took as they explored and settled what is now Idaho.

Miners and Mormons

In 1860, gold was discovered on Orofino Creek in northern Idaho. Miners poured into the region trying to make their fortune. Meanwhile, settlers had started arriving to farm the grasslands of southern Idaho. Many of them were Mormons, members of a religious group that had faced **persecution** in the East. Soon, southern Idaho was dotted with Mormon settlements.

Miners reached the depths of their underground workplaces by traveling in rail cars.

Troubled Times

As more settlers arrived, the animals that Shoshone hunted for food disappeared. The starving Shoshone sometimes raided the new farms for food. Hostilities increased. In 1863, U.S. Army forces attacked a Shoshone camp on Bear River in southeastern Idaho. They killed hundreds of Shoshone women, men, and children. It was the worst **massacre** of Native Americans in U.S. history.

Timeline of Idaho Events

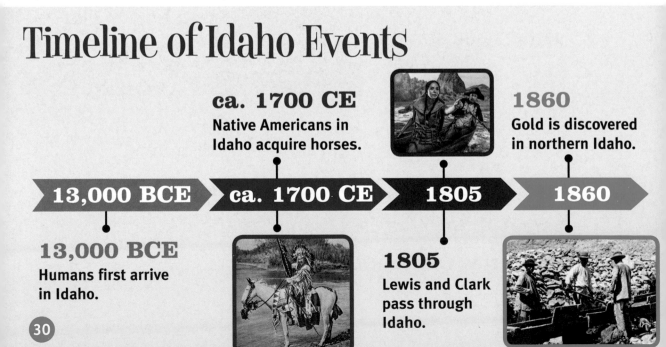

ca. 1700 CE
Native Americans in Idaho acquire horses.

1860
Gold is discovered in northern Idaho.

13,000 BCE ca. 1700 CE 1805 1860

13,000 BCE
Humans first arrive in Idaho.

1805
Lewis and Clark pass through Idaho.

Statehood and Beyond

Idaho developed quickly in the later 19th century. The first railroad reached Idaho in the 1870s. Cities such as Boise and Moscow grew. In 1890, with a population of about 90,000, Idaho became the 43rd U.S. state. Logging and mining boomed. Miners worked in dangerous conditions for little pay. Violence often broke out as they tried to force mine owners to improve safety and wages.

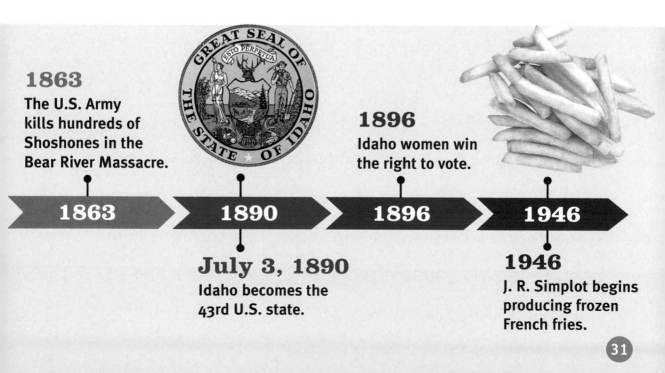

1863
The U.S. Army kills hundreds of Shoshones in the Bear River Massacre.

1896
Idaho women win the right to vote.

1863   1890   1896   1946

July 3, 1890
Idaho becomes the 43rd U.S. state.

1946
J. R. Simplot begins producing frozen French fries.

Many of Idaho's farm families suffered during the 1930s.

More Recent Times

The 1930s were hard for Idahoans. The country had entered an economic **depression**. Many businesses closed, so people lost their jobs. The U.S. government began programs to help. In Idaho, one program brought electricity to remote towns and farms that did not have it. Later in the 20th century, Idaho's farms and industries thrived. The state grew as people moved there for work and to enjoy its rugged wilderness.

The Potato King

By the mid-20th century, Idaho led the nation in the production of potatoes. John Richard Simplot wanted to make the potatoes easier to ship around the country. In 1946, the J. R. Simplot Company began producing frozen French fries. Simplot supplied the fries to grocery stores and later fast-food chains such as McDonald's. Simplot's work revolutionized Idaho industry. Today, more than 60 percent of Idaho potatoes are **processed** before they are shipped out of state.

A worker tests a French fry during a quality inspection at an Idaho potato processing plant.

At the annual Shoshone-Bannock Pow Wow, Native Americans from around the country gather in Idaho to celebrate cultural traditions.

CHAPTER 4

Culture

Many people move to Idaho to find peace and quiet amid the beautiful scenery. Some of them are writers. In the 1950s, Ernest Hemingway moved to Idaho. He was one of the nation's most celebrated authors. Award-winning writer Marilynne Robinson is from Sandpoint. Many kinds of musical events are popular in the state, from symphonies to fiddling festivals.

On the Fields and Slopes

Idahoans love football. They cheer for college teams like the University of Idaho Vandals and the Boise State Broncos. Idahoans also like to play sports. In the summer they golf, and in the winter they ski and snowboard. Sun Valley, in central Idaho, is a world-famous ski resort. The world's first ski lift was built there in 1936.

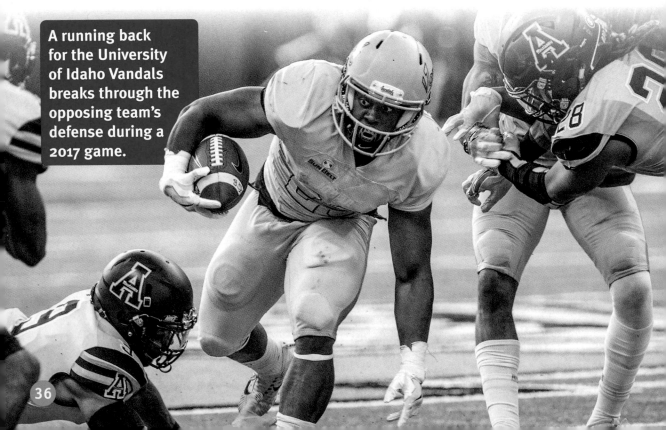

A running back for the University of Idaho Vandals breaks through the opposing team's defense during a 2017 game.

Celebrate

Fun events draw Idaho neighbors together throughout the year. People build giant snow sculptures at the Winter Carnival in McCall. Colorful hot-air balloons fill the sky at the Teton Valley Balloon Rally in Driggs. Some Idaho festivals connect the state's past and present. The Trailing of the Sheep Festival in Sun Valley recalls Idaho's sheep-ranching history. Native Americans gather at the Shoshone-Bannock Indian Festival for traditional dances and other events.

More than 60,000 people visit the McCall Winter Carnival each year.

Special machines are used to pick potatoes and shake them free of dirt before they are dumped in a truck and transported away from the fields.

At Work

People in Idaho work in a wide variety of jobs. Some are farmers who grow crops such as wheat and potatoes. Idaho produces about a third of all the nation's potatoes. Some Idahoans are miners or loggers. Others work in factories, making everything from canned fruit to computer parts. Tourism is booming in Idaho, so lots of people go to work in restaurants and ski resorts.

From Food to Computers

For decades, Idaho's biggest industry was food processing—turning crops into packaged food. But the world has changed, and so has Idaho. Today, Idaho's leading industry is technology. Computer chips, printers, and other tech goods are all made in Idaho. In fact, Idaho's technology sector is growing so fast that there sometimes aren't enough people to fill all the jobs!

Students in Boise make adjustments to a robotics project.

Let's Eat

Idaho food is delicious and filling. Idahoans eat a lot of potatoes, but they also enjoy all sorts of other foods. Huckleberries are the state fruit. They are great on ice cream. Many Idahoans love to fish, so trout is often on the menu. Basque croquetas are balls of fried bread crumbs filled with meat, cheese, or potatoes.

 ## Mashed Potatoes

Ask an adult to help you!

These tasty potatoes make a great side dish.

Ingredients
2 pounds potatoes
Salt
2 tablespoons butter
1 cup milk
Pepper

Directions
Peel the potatoes and cut them into quarters. Fill a pot with water and add salt. Bring the water to a boil, then add the potatoes. Cook them for 20 minutes, or until they are tender. Meanwhile, in a small pan, heat the butter and milk over low heat. Drain the potatoes and then mash them. Stir in the milk and butter mixture. Add salt and pepper to taste. Enjoy!

Mountain biking is a popular activity in many of Idaho's outdoor areas.

Out and About

In Idaho, people can take raft trips down white-water rivers and go on hikes through rocky canyons. They can also spend time fishing. There's nothing better than wading into a river in the quiet of the morning and casting a line. While waiting for a bite, you can take in the wilderness around you. You may not be lucky enough to catch a trout. But you're lucky to be in Idaho. ★

Famous People

Sacagawea

(1786?–1812), a Shoshone Native American, was born in what is now central Idaho. She worked as a **translator** for Lewis and Clark as they traveled across the West to the Pacific Ocean.

Gutzon Borglum

(1867–1941), from Bear Lake, sculpted the faces of four presidents on Mount Rushmore in South Dakota. He and his assistants spent 14 years creating the huge sculpture.

Carol Ryrie Brink

(1895–1981) wrote several classic novels for children. They include *Caddie Woodlawn*, which won the Newbery Medal for the year's best children's book. She grew up in Moscow.

Philo Farnsworth

(1906–1971) was an inventor. While still in high school in Rigby, he worked out a design for an early television.

Lana Turner

(1921–1995) was one of the most popular actors of the 1940s and 1950s. She appeared in such films as *The Postman Always Rings Twice* and *Imitation of Life*. She was from Wallace.

Harmon Killebrew

(1936–2011) was a baseball player known for his powerful hitting. He hit 573 home runs during his Major League career. He was from Payette.

Victor Wooten

(1964–) is a Grammy Award–winning musician who is widely considered one of the greatest bass players of all time. He was born in Mountain Home.

Kristin Armstrong

(1973–) is a professional bicycle racer who lives in Boise. She won gold medals at the Olympics in 2008, 2012, and 2016.

Christina Hendricks

(1975–) is an actor from Twin Falls. She is best known for her performance on the TV show *Mad Men*. She earned six Emmy nominations for her work on the show.

Bryan Fuller

(1969–) is a television writer and producer. He has created such shows as *Pushing Daisies*, *Hannibal*, and *American Gods*. He was born in Lewiston.

Aaron Paul

(1979–) is an award-winning actor from Boise. He is famed for his work on such TV shows as *Breaking Bad*, *BoJack Horseman*, and *The Path*.

Did You Know That ...

Idaho's capitol is heated by **geothermal** water. Hot water is brought up from deep underground and piped throughout the building. The heat from the water spreads, warming the building.

Idaho is a made-up word. When the U.S. government was dividing up land in the West, a businessman suggested it as a name. He said it was a Shoshone word meaning "gem of the mountains," but it wasn't true!

A church called the Cataldo Mission is the oldest building in Idaho. It was built in 1853.

Let's name the state IDAHO! It means "gem of the mountains"! (I think)

That's a great name!

In the 1860s, many Chinese people moved to Idaho to search for gold. By 1870, one out of every four people in Idaho was Chinese.

The word *potatoes* was first mentioned on Idaho license plates in 1928. It was used on and off for many years. Since 1957, the plates have said "famous potatoes."

Did you find the truth?

(T) Idaho produces more potatoes than any other state.

(F) European Americans began settling Idaho in the 1700s.

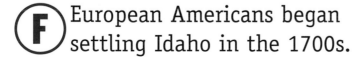

Resources

Books

Edgar, Sherra G. *What's Great About Idaho?* Minneapolis: Lerner, 2015.

Jazynka, Kitson. *Sacagawea.* Washington, DC: National Geographic, 2015.

Krull, Kathleen. *The Boy Who Invented TV: The Story of Philo Farnsworth.* Decorah, IA: Dragonfly Books, 2014.

Rozett, Louise (ed.). *Fast Facts About the 50 States: Plus Puerto Rico and Washington, D.C.* New York: Children's Press, 2010.

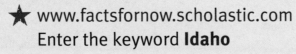

Visit this Scholastic website for more information on Idaho:
★ www.factsfornow.scholastic.com
Enter the keyword **Idaho**

Important Words

depression (dih-PRESH-uhn) a time when the economy of a country is shrinking and many people lose their jobs

geothermal (jee-oh-THUR-muhl) of or having to do with the heat inside the earth and its commercial use

horticulture (HOR-ti-kuhl-chur) the science of growing flowers, fruits, and vegetables

massacre (MAS-uh-kur) the violent killing of a large number of people at the same time, often in battle

missionaries (MISH-uh-ner-eez) people who are sent to a foreign country to teach about religion and do good works

persecution (pur-suh-KYOO-shuhn) the continued treatment of someone in a cruel or unfair way, especially because of that person's ideas or political beliefs

processed (PRAH-sest) prepared or changed by a series of steps

territory (TER-ih-tor-ee) an area connected with or owned by a country that is outside the country's main borders

tipis (TEE-peez) tentlike dwellings made by stretching animal skins across a wooden frame

translator (TRANZ-lay-tur) someone who changes words from one language to another language

Index

Page numbers in **bold** indicate illustrations.

About the Author

Melissa McDaniel is the author of more than thirty books for young people. She was born in Portland, Oregon, and attended both Portland State University and the University of Washington. She now lives in New York City, where she works as a writer and editor.